VOICES & VENUES In VERSE!

Choices, Chances & Life!

By -
Kenneth J. Hesterberg

Copyright © 2018 by Kenneth J. Hesterberg

All rights reserved.

ISBN 978-1-62806-197-0

Library of Congress Control Number 2018xxxxxx

Published by Salt Water Media
29 Broad Street, Suite 104
Berlin, MD 21811
www.saltwatermedia.com

Cover image courtesy P/Lt. Lawrence G. Davies,
Cambridge Sail and Power Squadron
Interior image of lighthouse origin is a public domain image
taken by United States Coast Guard

Rationale!

Life *is a Gift,*
<u>*Choices*</u>*; are what you make,*
<u>*Chances*</u>*; are, what you take__*
To make life,
Worth the time and effort,
Between__ birth and demise!

Simple it sounds,
Not so, when facing each day!
There, will always be,
Something or Someone,
Putting obstacles in your way!

So, what does makes, "Life Interesting?"

<u>CHALLENGES!</u>

Make it, worthwhile getting up__
In the morning, each day!
And, living fully__
While, its your time, on earth__ to stay!

Dedication

How many people have I met in my lifetime__ thus far?
How many more, to meet before in life I retire?
To the former, a guess of 10,000, I'd say!
To the latter, God's choice to convey!
In season, 100 holiday letters send!
Less in each year__ gone away!
Many faces, I nay remember!
But, each in life played a role!
All, part of what I am today!
So gratitude__ to all send!
And, a wish we meet,
Some place,
In__ time__
Together,
Again__!
Perhaps,
Then can,
Thank every one of them?

Hallmark of the Chesapeake Bay!

Iconic, somewhat historic!
Was not one, but many!
Few, remain in service this day,
Most, at museums found,
Reminders of another time!

"**The Bay**" and its lights__
And, Lighthouses!
My Muse!
(The inspiring power of Poetry- Verse!)
Mine, since a lad of youth!

Choices: alternatives, preferences, select ability!
Chances: luck, fortuitous opportunities!
Life: the state of actual living!

""They__ the Sub Title, of this Anthology!

Table of Contents

Prologue 13

Life-Long Trait? 14

The Simplicity of Life! 14

The Gamble 15

The Pond! 16

Dollars, Cents & Sense! 17

A Time of Opining! 18

Factors Exposed! 20

Old Friends! 21

Think! 22

Contemplation 23

A Train to School! 24

Genius! 25

Luck! 26

Perhaps! 27

Just Thoughts! 28

In Review! 29

Where, Talent Lay! 30

In Gratitude! 31

One That Got Away! 32

A Debt Owed! 34

Hope For a Better, World? 35

Generational Thoughts! 36

Ancestors – Ours! 37

What To Do? 38

Wishing Doesn't Make it!	39
Options? Choices?	40
Repetition!	41
The Answer is, "Within!	42
The Last Game!	43
Conversation With Self!	44
My Favorite Season!	46
My Love, My Life!	47
Paddle Days!	48
Concept!	50
Reflections!	51
Vicissitudes!	52
Change?	54
A Thought to Heed!	55
Truth Be Mine!	56
Hear Me Please!	57
A Lesson Reviewed!	58
Reminder!	59
Life Reviewed!	60
Keep 10% in Tact!	61
Humankind on Trial!	62
Is the Past the Future?	65
Sextet of the Xmas Season	66
Christmas Twenty-Seventeen!	66
#2 My Christmas Confession!	68
3 Natures, Xmas Song!	69
#4 The Christmas Gift!!	70

#5 Belief!	71
$6 One Christmas Eve Night	72
Ah, Seasons Four	73
Those Left Behind!	74
Just a Thought!	75
City Kid!	76
ABoat!	79
Nonsensical, Suppositions!	80
Of a Man Known!	82
Doubling Down!	84
A Timely Thought!	86
Question?	87
Pain Be Real!	87
To Each Ones' Own!	88
Your Choice!	89
Gratitude & Sorrow!	90
Then and Now!	91
Death be Damned!	92
To Listen!	94
Why?	96
From the Vineyard!	97
Facing Life!	98
Music of its Time!	100
A, Thought to Think!	101
Pros & Cons!	102
Words Never Said!	103
Benediction for Boaters!	104

Prologue

After writing a number of books,
That, some call poetry?
I have begun to think, they are, more, a series__
Of, <u>Short Stories</u>, written in Verse!

<u>Verse</u> to me, is not,
A novel, to read cover to cover!
And, then left to collect dust, on a shelf!
But rather, like and old friend,
You remember, and on whom make a call!

With the book in hand,
You peruse the Table of Contents!
Like, two old friends chatting!
Topics, you pick and choose!
Then in the book you, select one__
To suit your, fancy, at the time!
Hopefully immerse yourself,
In the words and rhythms,
That not only you enjoy,
But, may open your mind__
To diverse subjects and ideas!

I do hope you open this book__
On many occasions, and, it serves you well!
Wishing you and yours, the very best!

- kjh

Φ

Life-Long Trait?

Truth, a double-sided knife!
Edges sharp__ cuts with no report!
White lies__ egos to support!
Real truth, sometimes good,
Sometimes, cuts to the quick!

Truth, so important,
Keep's ones' integrity "in tact,"
Lies, caught__ digs a grave__ in fact!
So, truth can make or break,
Even the best life-long pact!

Truth, the chance for those__
With a strong will and heart!
Knowing, the telling can hurt,
Still and always,
Tells the truth, never, ever departs!

Φ

The Simplicity of Life!

I sure enjoy the sunrise,
When, green grass, I can see,
And, its color is not brown,
Another day, there is__ for me,
Time__ to put my feet upon the ground!
And enjoy, every earthly sound!

Φ

The Gamble!

Loaned times; borrowed by we,
God's investment in humankind!
The Master took the chance__
To breathe life in you and me!

Good, bad or indifferent,
Has it, paid a dividend?
Or, is it a loss__
On, heaven's Income Sheet?

There must be times,
When the bill will arise,
Are, tears show in God's eyes?
For, our waste and stupidity!

How long must the Master wait?
For humankind, his, plan to make?
We, his children, must frustrate__
More, than even__ his patience can take!

Will it ever be so?
That, humankind, truly appreciates?
All, that the Master, dedicates,
In, making life on Earth__ an Eden for us?

Or, is the time now near?
When Nature, this World will clear__
All humankind, from far and near,
And, only devastation__ will appear?

Φ

The Pond!

I gazed at the Pond within my sight,
The breeze was blowing, left to right!
The sunlit trees, and cat-o-nine tails,
Swaying their heads, the sky impaled!

The morning was bright,
The sky, with puff white clouds,
A peaceful vista, birds singing loud!
A picture true, of autumn delight!

Like as too, a woodland dream,
Birds dodging in this surround,
The coolness of the morning,
This tranquil scene and sound!

But let your eyes take in more,
And, one would spy a "Dollar Store."
The dream__ a "catch Pond"
Just to tend the site!

But, one could imagine,
The pond elsewhere,
If one could hold, vision direct,
See it! See it in a forest somewhere!

This urban site__
A compromise of the governing class!
Just, a bit of nature,
Out of place, but__ placed just right!

Φ

Dollars, Cents & Sense!

I know not, when?
My last day is to come?
For, if I did,
I would, save a tidy some!

And gather all those dollars in,
And, when the time came,
For me, my maker to meet,
I'd take them, for a coffin spin!
Piled and banded neatly within!

To the place, where ere I would go,
Those dollars, I would take to surely know,
Up or down, to be my place,
A, condo buy, for my space!
And, no landscaping__
I would face!
So, why not?
I shouldn't live in grace?
For all the trials and tribulations__
On Earth; that, I did face?

Hey! Just an amusing thought or two!
I know that God or the Devil will choose,
Be it up or down, my final place__
I hope it is up, where there must be more space?
For if most folks, are just like you?
Down__ must be a crowded zoo__
But, I'm sure Satin will save, a spot for you__
So, bye, bye and "Toddle-Lu!"

Φ

A Time of Opining!

I was just thinking, the other day,
About times, long gone away,
As, I looked upon a pocket watch,
That was my grandfather's__ in his day!

Like many other things,
I took for granted,
When the sun arose,
"Good Morning", to say!

That gold watch, in its case__ did lie!
On the coffee table,
In the family room,
As a centerpiece, for years on nigh!

Looking at that pocket watch,
On this particular day,
I thought of both grandfathers,
In the graves, where they lay!

Because, another birthday I did pass,
And, I saw that watch under its polished glass,
My thoughts did turn, to those relatives mine,
Whom I thought so old, in days behind!

And, it struck, me hard,
And struck me fast,
I was older now__
Then, when they breathed their last?

How, could they have looked__?
So old to me,
When in the mirror now,
That age__ I do not see?

I was 10, when the first did pass!
And, 13, when life, the other died,
And, now in my dotage years,
Visit I, both graves, that lie, near by!

I think of them,
And, other relatives that have passed,
Five generations,
Within distance walking, in fields of grass!

But, I will be the last,
To visit grave sites, of the past,
For, my family__ lives so far away!
In a State up north, to breathe each day!

But, this doesn't make me sad!
For my son, never knew,
His, great grand dads!
And that__ was their loss too!

So, I realize in wisdom gained,
That life, speeds on, like a rushing, train!
And, no portraits on walls we retain,
But, maybe in heaven, all family__ reclaimed?

Now, don't be morbid,
And, don't you be sad,
Just think perhaps a family tree, be had,
And, you meet those, who's DNA you share!

For, it doesn't hurt a bit,
To take some time,
And, think of those, you left behind,
They likely did the same__ in their time!

But do remember,
Because they were here,
You, had this chance,
For, a life to "steer!"

Yes, family is what we got,
Knew them well, or knew them not!
Like them__ maybe or maybe not!
But, they were all the family; you've got!

I hope these musings of mine,
Tickle, a spot in your mind,
And, someday soon, you take the time,
Too think of those__ you have left behind!

Φ

Factors Exposed!

The days of life__ are not known!
You throw the dice,
When birth be shown,
Ahead of you, are challenges grand!
Be you, woman or a man!

This just a reminder,
To keep you on your toes!
Because time is a precious gift,
So, let not a weakness you expose,
To cheat you of the time,
God for you, proposed!

Φ

Old Friends!

I met and dined,
With some folks the other day,
Whose husband and father,
That week had passed away!

It was like old times,
We, all once knew,
Except, one was missing,
And, a tear would arrive, on cue!

We talked of kids,
And grandkids too,
And, of other friends,
Alive, and some gone from view!
And, those many years long gone,
That, had slipped and slid away,
And, we knew, because of distance,
Few new gatherings would come our way,

I guess folks, whose age had come,
Must face the realization some,
That, memories do replace,
Get-togethers of another time and place!
And, I only hope and pray,
My memories stay clear,
Until, that final day,
When it's my turn to be on my way!

So, to those friends, I said good-bye,
Lets keep in touch, both you and I__
And we three had a final hug,
And, there was a tear in every eye!

And, I will try to ring their phone,
To let them know, they are not alone!
And, that I do remember,
Those good times__ from the bye and bye!

Φ

Think!

Should, I wake, tomorrow morn,
And, see the sun on the rise,
And, breathe the breath of life,
And, overcome my surprise,
That I am still alive?

With another day, before me then,
And, this chance to face the 24?
A time to grab new challenges,
That makes life worth__
This a gift from God,
I've been given once more!

As I have gotten older,
Each, additional minute, I obtain,
I look to what, I can do?
To, pay my dues?
For this day, and those before!
For each soul, owes a debt,
When first given, a Life to explore!

Ah, every day a glorious day, when one can rise,
And be on ones way!   What more to ask, what more to say?
Then to thank God __ for another day!

Φ

Contemplation!

Do you believe__ you can see,
In a dream, of something never known?

Details, later found to be true,
So, insane, it eats at you so?

How could a vision be?
Of things, once unknown, in a time before,
That are now are seen.
By one or some, or even more?

Are there many, who a seer would be?
Is there an entity, putting thoughts in thee?

Is this God's or an alien's wooing?
Or are some brains, much more able at doing?

If 10% of the brain we are only using,
What could be accomplished?
If more to use, were at our choosing?
Would the world be better, or just more abusing!

Just a few thoughts,
Perhaps quite amusing!

But, just suppose,
We reach say 90%, would /could, life be better spent?

Φ

A Train to School!

In the years gone by,
A group and I__
Would walk, those miles to school!

A short cut on the railroad tracks,
Was our daily trek?
Mostly going, but sometimes back!

The stepping from tie to tie,
Cut, distance and time,
Taken we, in rain or shine!

And, once in a while,
A train we "hopped",
To arrive, at our jumping off spot!

But, came a day, with Halloween done__
The train was stopped,
To allay, some trickster's fun!

The crew did clear, the cluttered track,
Then, us hanging on, the engine did move,
To get their schedule back!

That train didn't slow, as days before,
But with some speed rambled on!
And, jump we landed, on sand and thorn!

Bushed ourselves off, each of us did!
Gathered our books,
And up the hill, to school we sped!

That was the last time,
Together, we hopped a train,
Lesson learned - sanity gained!

Foolish kids, in early teens,
Yes, lesson learned,
Lucky, only scraps were seen!

I wonder if still alive?
Those old-friends remember that "ride?"
But, after, 70 years, maybe cobwebs they hide?

Φ

Genius!

Leonardo-- left this world at 67.
Just think to "turn" those years to 76?
Nine more years of brilliance!
In engineering and art, and math!

Additional wealth of knowledge untold,
So much more, would challenge__
The future of thought!

Oh, with near a decade more__
Perhaps, another Mona Lisa,
Could now this world find?
Ah, da Vinci, man of talent!
Will, there, ever be another__
To, grace this world of mine?

Φ

Luck!

Luck, is said to be,
The distillation, of work that is hard,
Some would disagree,
For, they see neighbors_ the lottery win?
But, who knows, how much work they put in?

But, the, lottery, is not of what I, speak!
That is a fortune_ few do see,
It is the daily effort, that most put in,
To meet the cost, of bills to pay,
That is what I am speaking of this day!

Now, where does luck come in?
Do, all have an equal share?
Is it something all, can depend upon?
Or, an intangible_
That disappears in thin air?

Yes, luck is something, all at one time see,
Sometimes bits and other times more to be!
But, must be recognized when it comes,
And, be accepted readily_
Or, it will pass right by thee!

Do you ever think, how truly lucky you are?
I am sure, good luck you have seen,
Did it not come after hard work?
Or, was work not in your dream?
Just hang on and see what I mean?

I know luck you have seen!
Were you, not born to chase a dream?
Did you not wake this morn?
And, green grass to see!
This and many more, for you to redeem!

Now true, some have more luck, and some less!
But, you must confess,
"Lady Luck", many times, shines on you!
Otherwise, deceased you be__ that is true!
So, work harder, possible, more luck to view!

Φ

Perhaps!

When in maturity you realize,
It matters not what you were?
But, with effort, what you did__ become!
It matters not, from where you came,
But, where you go__
Throughout your life, that all will know!

It matters not how far up__
The ladder you do climb,
But, how many you reach down,
To help, raise up__ in their time!
Forgiveness, for bad actions,
Some will not extend!
But, if you know, good you've become__
Then in your heart, no debts do owe__ to anyone!

Φ

Just Thoughts!

What do you do?
When, your love__ you lose?
Is there a time?
When you, again, must choose?

For me, I still wear__ my wedding ring,
For, she always,
Made my heart sing!
I needed no more, no fields to explore,
But I have friends,
Who made another choice!
And, I applaud their change of course!

Different strokes, for different folks!
That is the way, I do see!
Each__ must make a life choice,
To fit their time, and their course!

I miss my bride,
More than I can say,
I think of her, each and every day,
And, also when little things come my way!
I have this feeling__ this will always be?
And, that is okay, with me!
For, she was my light for thousands of nights,
And, nothing more is owed to me!

Now don't get me wrong,
For, I do love__ a female for company!
And, I share with them all,
Just how with me it will be!

You can love someone,
And not be in love!
The difference is emotion and chemistry!
So in friendship, there are no strings on me!

Me I look at love,
As, friendship and fairness,
And__ to help and enjoy,
With, companionship to share!
Will this be my fate, to employ?
Or, will there be more?
I know not,
But, time will add up the score!

If for me, there is to be more?
I will never leave good memories behind__
But, must leave old baggage to store,
And, make new, if there is more__ I am to find!

Φ

In Review!

Let your mind not be cluttered,
Cast out all negative thoughts,
To keep them is foolish__
For, how dearly retention cost!

The time you are granted,
Is measured in breaths!
Don't, waste even one!
You deserve__ only the best!

Φ

Where, Talent Lay!

Real talent__ is a nebulous thing!
Granted, to a percentage of the few!
No matter, what bell it rings,
Seldom do the beneficiaries realize__
That, theirs is a gift so true!
To them, perhaps, it was something due!

Look, at history all around,
And, note the transgressions,
Of most, who think it is their due,
Who imbibe in reckless behavior?
Who cut short their lives!
And, the talent, God gave them to do!
The list of those who wasted thus,
Is long and sorely fraught,
And many times hurts, those of us,
Who no talent, could be bought!
And, we then lose twice,
For what, perhaps was owed to us!

It is a shame__
Talent, we cannot pass down,
Like to an heir, of silver and gold!
But, that today, we cannot do,
But, who knows what in tomorrow,
New technology will unfold?
Say you, that talent, was theirs,
To do with what they wished?
And, that brings tears to my eyes,
For one thing you dismissed!
That talent was a Godly gift,
Like the Sun, to be shared by all!

And when their day is gone,
How many decades, must come to pass?
Before, we talentless millions have to wait,
For, another, like talent__
Would come to pass?
And, that too, is destined, to never last?

Φ

In Gratitude!

Alive, on borrowed time,
From birth to decline!
For me, this is fine!

For whatever, time is mine,
My goal will be,
To prepare, my Legacy!

This, to thank those,
Who, in there time;
Paved an easier way for me!

Should, you not, a legacy make?
For you and all, have a debt to repay__
For, the life given you,
And, a chance to live; even one day!

Φ

One That Got Away!

My short term memory, has gone astray,
Never, had to worry about it, in passed days!
But now, "dog-gone-it",
It has, become a plague to me!

You've heard the story of older folk,
Who hustle, to a room__?
With, an errand in mind,
And, then wonder why,
With a job to do, are, standing there,
Not knowing, what they are to find?

Now, I write a little verse in time,
And, often wake in the night
With, some lines in mind,
And, I quickly do get up,
To, write them down,
So, in the morning, they can be found!

Now, this I've done for many a year,
Many nights, lost sleep, I fear,
But, if I don't, those words are smoke--
That by sunlight, do disappear,
Never recaptured, no matter__
How hard, my, mind, I stroke!

Now one day, not long ago,
I, was driving to a place I know,
And, words of a verse,
They came to me,
Full and sweet, as they could be!
And, I swore they wouldn't get away!

But, when I did stop, not far away,
Gone they were, just like nighttime smoke,
I'm telling you, this, "ain't" no joke!
I've thought and thought,
And, tried to capture them, too write it down,
But, not one word, for me is found!

That verse__ was right on the spot!
So, I think this is what I've got to do?
Till, I reach my burial time__
From now on, stop that car, on a dime?
And jot that verse on paper fine,
So, lost verses__ plague me not!

Then, I can get on, with what life I've got!
But, you know another idea is,
Get me a handheld recording machine,
Save those words__ when they are rum,
Because, I know if lost,
They will bug me, for weeks to come!

I know, and understand,
You think me nuts__ one crazy man!
But__ some day you might find,
What it is like, to lose something grand,
And, if like me; miserable, you will be__
With things, not under your command!

So, I am sharing this with you,
For someday, your short memory too,
Will take a hike, most likely true!
And, just maybe__
These timely tips,
Will keep you sane, at home or on auto trips!

Φ

A Debt Owed!

A, legacy is what we owe,
For, our time, granted on this orb,
And, to those, who paved our way!
Who, left for us, the stepping-stones,
To make easier, our every day!

Yes, recognition, we should bestow,
To those who came before!
And, to honor them, with our legacy,
Bye leaving it, for generations more,
As was done, in all millennia before!

True, each and everyone,
Has a debt, from day of birth,
And, the conscientious, will accept this,
While a number__ this, onus will desert!
Choices seen, till the end of days on Earth!

But, you are a child of God,
So, the choice is yours__
To do, what you know you should,
And, help assure a better__ future world,
Or, spend eternity__ with the Devil, you could!

Some of humankind__ never see,
That life is a gift, loaned to thee!
That, theirs is a debt to repay__
To leave Earth__ an even better place,
Then first, we did see!

Φ

Hope for a Better, World?

Grateful am I, for verse I pen,
And, nice words I hear in praise,
And, glad too, that I can aid,
Non-Profit- groups, that my books do use,
To acquire funds, for efforts they do!

But sadness I feel,
That my parents and "bride",
Lost the breath of life,
And, never did see, books from me,
That I have written, in later life!

To write I did in my professional days,
And, while verse over the years did pen,
It wasn't until my "bride" did pass,
That more writing,
And, publishing, I did extend!

My wife, knew many bits of verse,
On Christmas, family letters I wrote,
But, even she would have been surprised,
At the amount__ I now compose,
But, can never orally quote.

I truly hope, my words once written,
Will help many, who peruse the lines,
And perhaps, open their minds,
To, what they too can do__
With, a pencil or pen__ and some time!

Φ

Generational Thoughts!

When young I was,
I thought young, I would always be!
And, while, I saw old about,
I felt, that would never be me!

But now, here I am,
Looking back on life,
With, some time that spans__
Across two centuries, in this land!
Now, hear me__ I am complaining not,
I have had a life,
That many others,
So wished, they, my life had got!

But in age, I've seen,
Many lives__ as a book not yet bound!
Some of those lives; are a mystery,
Others__ are as open, as found!

I will not bore you, with my chronology,
True, there would be some passages__
Perhaps be worth your time__ to read?
But, it is time for more living__ that you need!
However, there is a reason,
I bring, these thoughts to you__
It is a challenge, for you to do, what I did do__
Begin jotting lines__ that come to you!

And should, this you do?
Some type of legacy, could outline?
A gift, a history, a bit of love,
For those to come, who will follow you!

Perhaps, this has never entered your mind?
This, was me, until I did find__
There was much__ I wanted to leave behind,
That, most of my ancestors__ had declined!
How much of them, I wish I knew,
And, of the centuries long gone by,
Of things done and undone,
That, they did or wished they had tried!

Φ

Ancestors – Ours!

When it is my time__
My resting place, will be,
Near five generations of family!
Maybe__ then since, I be not far away.
Those born before my dying day,
Their spirits, will gather round,
And, many, many stories relay!

Crazy thought__ you might be right,
But, think just what tales,
Those spirits, could relate!
And, those others in nearby__ States,
Not too far away__ could participate!

Yes, many more ancestors, here and about,
What history, what facts__
Of life and times, to know at last!
Think to take you the time, to look into,
The lineage, of those__
Whose DNA, they shared with you!

Φ

What To Do?

I don't understand this world today!
When young, it could have been the same?
But, then, I was just a kid,
And, my desire was to go out and play!

Now: however_ the chaos today,
Puts, actual fear into me,
Too many people,
With angst, ruining the nights away!

Can we return things?
To, what they should be?
Can we, the living today_
Bring back the sanity of yesterday?

How did we the people,
Let, our county get this way?
Or, is the devil,
With, his hands of cards_ at play?

Is there a chance?
With diligence and hard work,
We once more_ will find better days?
Days, where we respect, other's ways?

Hear this prayer,
Oh Heavenly father,
Chastise us, but let us not be,
The last generation_ of this country free!

Φ

Wishing Doesn't Make it!

For, you I wish__
You, "make" each day,
The very best it can be!
But, this is a wish, not a gift!
So, some thought; is required by thee!

You, must understand, only you,
Can "Make" each day, the best__ it can be,
For, to "have"__ a good day,
Means, someone must__
Bestow that gift, on thee?

And perhaps__ some could give,
To you a gift__ that "good" would be,
But, most, preface "good" with "have a,"
When, on their way, out the door__
As they go, to flee!

Tis up to you, and only you,
To "make", a good day__ become true!
You cannot, stand around and wait,
For then__
Only age, will you accrue!

I hope these words, hit home,
And, make sense__ good and clear,
For, in everyday, that comes your way,
Opportunities do appear!
And, "make" is "the course," you must steer!

Φ

Options? Choices?

Choices__ never take a break!
Choices__ so many each day to make!
Choices__ Right? Wrong? Either? Or!
Choices__ no ducking them__ for sure?

The point? No one tells you true?
That, from birth to death__
No matter, what else you do,
Your life is ruled by choice__
And, this is a fact, for you!

You "must" prepare yourself_
Mentally, psychologically, physically__
For each "choice" to make,
Many times this is automatic,
A brain function, for granted you take!

But, when taken for granted__
You think the right choice,
You will make__
Many times, that is a big mistake!

For the bigger the opportunity__
The better the chance,
Of, your choice be wrong,
Then, sing you the moaner's song!

Perhaps, split second,
Is all it takes; or will take?
To, study the question, or the options?
Before a wrong choice, you will make!

So reflect!
Options: are opportunities!
Choices: Selection for action!
If you don't consider them both,
Your life___ may end up, in traction!

Φ

Repetition!

History, while in the past__
Many times__ is a future forecast!
Of what again__ will come!
Think not this, and you are dumb!
For humankind__ learns not,
What history teaches__ well,
And, through the ages gone!
The horror of "War"__ never, loses its smell!

And, skipping a generation or less,
Man, his saber's rattle,
And the young, like cattle,
Are, led to the slaughter__ in battle!

But, what is this fascination,
For some to follow__
A, Sociopaths, invitation?
Whereby death, reduces many__
Of the unknown, best of that generation!
Will this "stupidity" never stop?
Will all, never realize, to recapture Eden__
Full brotherhood__ must rule each season?

Φ

The Answer is, "Within!"

God__
Do you believe, he or she, to be?
Say you no, then hear this old saw:
War, in fox- holes, no atheist there be!
Found during eons of battles,
The dying are heard to call,
For God or Mother,
Not the devil at all!

Today, with education fine,
Many; are claiming;
That the Bible is perhaps a good history__
From, the past and extended down through time!
And, no belief in God__ can they find?
What do you think?
Do you have a faith; you can define?

Perhaps, as bad as War is,
Or, any other__ fear found,
Maybe, if all had to dodge bullets,
Most would find,
Tis God, they call on in time?

Yes, perhaps it takes,
The taste of fear,
To open everyone's mind__
That there is a God!

Again, I ask? Do you believe, in the Devine?

Φ

The Last Game!

When the days count down,
And, age takes its toll,
You then realize,
Things you once tried,
Are not, again, to be challenged,
For they are, no longer your prize!

Tis, time, to step back,
And, let another in,
You felt the time was coming,
And, know now, the "fix" is in!

So, now, make the best of each day!
Let, another, hear the drum be played!

Take your place out of the line,
For, there is much left for you to find!

New is, for you to do, and try!
Those days you did seek glory,
Are, the times now gone by!
But, when asked advice__ you can supply!

Each and all, have somewhat their day!
Fifteen minutes of fame, more or less, arrayed!
But, all need to realize,
Time__ will close every door,
So, a new, challenge, one must tackle__
If life, tomorrow__ is to be explored!

Φ

Conversation With Self!

I understand, it is Nature's way,
To age us__ as we walk, along life's path!
But, do our bodies have to become,
The ogre, we see in the mirror's glass?

Why, can we not have back?
The body, we wore in days gone by?
And, those hormones,
That put that twinkle, in our eyes?

And, instead, of gray on my head,
Why not hair, that has life, and shine instead?
And, why those many wrinkles__
More each day__ that never ever go away!

And, why with experience,
So, vast and fine,
Why can I not, an heir to find?
To leave a legacy, so nothing be lost in time?

And, why now that I have the time,
Can I not, cast off all illness__?
Now, coming to my door?
To enjoy life; when no time, I had before?

With, so much more, I would like to do?
Did, I do something wrong?
That now, with little effort,
I hear the "Grim Reaper's" song?

I would guess, these question,
All, "gray heads;" in time do ask?
When they realize, at long last,
More time, is an un-purchasable thing to buy!

Oh, well_ so many details need doing,
So much, to ensure, before the going,
So, much left__ I want to see!
Is there time, for a "bucket list" for me?

I trust I did the best I could,
And, treated all, the way I should?
And, helped some others,
Travel up the ladder with me?

I do hope and pray,
Brave, I be__ all the way,
And, pray to God he make it fast,
When it's to be, my very last!

But, I m not ready, yet to go!
I have to get off my butt,
And, let others know__
I still have a bit of life to live!

But, who am I, to call the shot,
Just a human, a God, am not!
My time is in another's hands,
But, my good-byes; are at my command!

Well, thank you__ for this little talk!
A lot, I've to do, in my days yet to walk!
And, if good health, God grants to me,
More than a bucket list, the world I want to see!

Φ

My Favorite Season!

All kids__ like summer!
When school is closed up tight,
And, those long lazy days,
When playing and swimming, are in sight!

And, I too did like summer,
Particularly nearing my twelfth year,
WWII was over,
And with a cousin in PA, spent time so dear!

But, it was in that September,
And 12, I did become,
And, I joined Boy Scouting,
My, first big goal was won!

And, the first camping adventure,
Was in October time,
And, I will never forget the season and place!
And, the autumn leaves, colored find!

For at that moment,
I knew at once,
This season was to be mine,
This was my muse, I did find!

I loved the fall, to hike and all,
Or paddling a river down,
Or mountain trails, or sailing,
Before, winter's cold was around!

I married my bride,
On October's ides,
And, we traveled, most every fall!
That was, to us, when vacations__ would call!

It seems through my life,
Autumn, with its color rife,
Gave me, visions to keep,
Remembrances, of a season so right!

While other seasons I do like,
But, autumn's warm days and cool nights
And, colors, from God's pallet bright,
Is, and always will be__ my delight!

There is so much more,
Of my autumns, we could explore,
But, I am sure you now understand,
Fall, is my muse__ my heart's demand!

Ф

My Love, My Life!

I knew before teen years,
She was the love of my life,
She was to out-live me!
But, that wasn't to be!
And, here I stay,
Missing, her more everyday!
There, had to be a reason?
I am, yet, to find why__ I am here,
And she; too soon, gone on her way!

Ф

Paddle Days!

(Circa 1971 – 1976)
Co-ed Explorer Post 359
St. John's Lutheran Church, Linthicum, MD
(Parts and pieces of those yearly trips logged here.)

I can nay forget,
Those glorious days, now gone__
When a paddle was in my hands!
And, streams, and rivers and Bays,
Provided a venue, at my demand!
I remember best__ the 70's
In that century last,
And, the co-ed Explorer Post,
And, those teen-age adults,
Who kept me young, for the task!

Many names, from my mind now gone,
But faces, I'll see to my last!
And, they now mostly grand parents,
Only a few, I would know,
If, on the street, I would pass!

We taught them to paddle,
On a pond in town,
And, then at DC's Angler's Inn,
And then, to the moving__ Deer Creek,
Before, a down-river vocation to begin!
We sold hot dogs at E. J. Korvete's,
For, dollars, to fill our trailer's stock!
And, added more to the treasury,
Serving pancakes at St. J's!
For an ever growing flock!

Year round, we were on the water,
On rivers in many states!
And, skills were growing exponentially,
Many times in weather, with skies agape!

Each summer was a trip to Maine,
To test the Allagash River there,
And to cross into Canada,
On the St. John's river__ a paddler's lair!
We would drive north on a Friday night,
Changing drivers as we go,
All the teens of age,
Stick sifts to use, they, got to know!

Adventures, on these drives __would have,
Cars that sometime would refuse to go,
Or a trailer, needed welding__
So in Bridgeport, we got to know!

Then a night at Brunswick Naval Air Station,
Great breakfast before on our way!
Then on to Patton, Maine,
To the Lumberman's museum, and lunch,
Then that night at Lake Telos, we would stay,
And, there lots were drawn!
Of, who would drive the cars to St. Francis!
And fly back to meet us, on the river, below!

And, then in another year at Lake Telos__
Another welding, at a Lumber camp was done!
Maine's fine folks did help us!
And, with river projects, our appreciation did show!

Many adventures and stories__ are legend,
Like, sinking in the mud of the tramway,
And each year, never the same as the last!
But, would take pages and pages to relate!
Scribed here are just highlights,
Of, some of those days and nights!
Lucky I was, to know those young adults,
And to paddle the Allagash, a great delight!
And, share the experiences, and sights!

New, faces would replace, the old__
When, onto college they went!
Many, still keep in touch,
Sending photos of family, and such!

Near a-half century of time has passed! I see them in memories, strong,
As they were, those years ago! I hope they remember, those "Paddle Days"!
And, those times, when friendship did grow!

Φ

Concept!

Fairness, is a concept__
Nature, does not know!
Nurtured in humankind__
Untold millenniums__ ago!
Do you make decisions__ fairly?
When that is your job to do?
Remember, someone is watching you!

Φ

Reflections!

I write, because,
Lines of verse find me,
I write because I know,
If, I do not ink them down,
I will lose them__ forever,
For, I have never been able,
To remember or recite passages!
Yet, I can read what I have written,
And, know that I wrote it and when!
But not written, I lose them never to return!
It's like,
A big bell
Once rung!

With a,
Sound clear,
Pleasant, to the ear, worth, the time to hear!
For, you my Reader, I hope my verse, be__
Worth your time, & a great joy to heed,
And, within its lines, you do find,
Thoughts, once long repressed,
But, now__ joyously, found!
Yours_ your life to possess!
May all verse, nee poetry,
Hopefully__ mine, too,
Meet u'r desires!

Φ

Vicissitudes!

I thought once, of life__ forward,
And, no sense could I make,
For, my past, and, its memories,
Took hold, and crowded__ all the space!

Those memories I did conjure,
Of times, and people__ and places,
And, things of deep regard,
Were, moments painted in colors vivid,
Seen in detail, as though happening,
That moment, that instant,
Not in times, only__
When youth, was the trump card!

But, I know it's in the future,
Where the rest of life, makes its mark!
Those moments are just memories,
Mostly truth, but some fiction__
That your ego, initiates to start!

Ah, the future,
A shadow time, one must discern,
Unless one is a Seer,
Who sees, each tomorrow?
And, needs no time to learn!
But, in truth__ isn't the future,
Just an enigma, a conundrum,
A puzzle__
With, un-joined scattered pieces,
Just waiting, to play their part?

Or, are you one?
Who builds a plan, for tomorrow?
An engineer, of both time, and space?
Who, rallies up your forces?
And, bets each day be thine?

Or, are you one of the many,
Who cannot adapt,
To the vagaries, of the others;
Whose thoughts and actions__
Are not so inclined?

Yes, the future screams__
For, flexibility from an agile mind!
For, one who can influence,
Those tomorrows, if in tomorrow__
You even hope to reside?
Yes, now I know,
Tomorrow, is the utopia?
And, I must put my memories aside,
Only, bring them forward,
After, I dutifully step aside!

I once thought of life forward,
And all the effort__
Those many tomorrows would take?
But, changed my mind__
To, determine, I will become a Politician?

So, no, new thoughts,
I will ever need to make!
I'd love living on the Taxpayers dollar__
And watch the future taking place,
Bingo! Vicissitudes: this for me, and is no mistake!

Φ

Change?

Weapons from days of yore,
Changed with the winds of the time!
So, they now kill and maim more,
But, isn't killing still a crime?

Whose fault is war?
Has it changed from eons before?
Who are the guilty ones?
Do they burn in hell, for sure?

Those that are responsible,
Are, they Sociopaths, or psychopaths?
Of "paths"__ we haven't mapped?
Or__ even traveled before?

Or, what about those,
Who design, or manufacture,
Or, sell the weapons,
To, maim and kill so many more?

Should not they, be brought to task?
Should they not share the woe__?
Of, every mothers son,
Wounded in a field, or life again never know?

And, what about the politicians,
Who sign away the lives?
And, vote the youth to die?
Shouldn't they in pain__ be, made to cry?

Is the human race so immoral?
That war is inflected on all?
Why, can't we live in brotherhood?
Is that an option, too hard a call?

Hasn't mankind, seen war is for naught?
No one truly wins__ in battles fought!
Can we not change and make life fine,
Or, is this never to be__ but a dream of humankind?

Φ

A Thought To Heed!

And, a fine morning to you, "good person"!
And I pray you stay one step in front of the devil__
When it comes time, to dash to the Pearly Gates!

Remember, those gates be locked!
And, the key, can be found only while__
Living, "the Golden Rule!"
But know, should you do__
Your Guardian Angel,
Will bar__ the Devil from the gate__
When the Grim Reaper, pays his final call!

So live a good life, and keep fit, for that final run!
But, the good news is__ either up or down,
Some, of your friends__
Will be there, to welcome you in__ AMEN!

Φ

Truth Be Mine!

Never a master,
Of, the language English!
On my Bride, of near six decades,
I did rely!

For, she was, truly a Master,
And in agreement was I.
For she knew grammar,
And, how to make it apply!
But, to raise a line of verse,
That my Master; gave to me,
This an opportunity, to be his scribbler__
And that, I was proud to be!

And, then I'd call my bride,
And, with a smile she's read my lines,
And, mark in red, my many errors,
And, then "the Verse", would come out fine!

And, I 'd use those little red marks,
To learn, a bit more each time,
But, I was never as good as she!
And, I miss her, all the time!

Now, there are times,
When I am not so sure,
If, writing verse__
Is, a boon__ or a curse!
For, when in the night,
I must rise in the dark,
To capture, and ink the lines in my mind,
Or, have them lost__ never again to find!

Yes, verse is now my passion,
For, I can no longer__
Do, the many physical things__
I once attempted before!
But, those memories,
And, other new memories,
Give me fodder,
For wonders, I now do store!

Life, and my Master,
I feel demands, a pen be in my hand,
And, I but hope__ what I write,
Helps, many a living woman and man!

If that, which I pen,
Be accepted; as my legacy__
For, the living and beyond,
I then believe; I have heeded his command!

How, much more I am to write,
I nary have a clue? Tis, a decision of my Master__
And, readers__ such as you!

Φ

Hear Me Please!

I have, concern for each generation,
For they have come to believe, freedom is their right?
Not, understanding, in life__
For Freedom, others had to fight!
As, does, every generation__ or it be stolen, in the night!

Φ

A Lesson Reviewed!

LIFE: A sentence of hurt, pain, loss,
Subjugation, frustration,
Intimidation, slavery, retribution,
And, a few dozen more to name!

Or, on the other hand –
Love, family, friends, freedom, wealth,
Health, school, & more__ are gifts, for sure!

But, Nature is at work!
Eat or be eaten! Fight or flight!
Win, lose or draw?
But, also: the beauty of mountain,
Valley, seaside, streams forest, river, and more!

Death: a possibility is waiting?
As, is peace, to eternity_?
Is it God's, or the devil's call?

Yes, war or peace, parceled out__
Seldom? Never all at once be seen?
Selfishness, sociopaths, psychopaths,
Thieves, dictators, Kings, despots,
Mafia chiefs, heroes, and cowards!
And every once in while__
Honest men, but too few of these?

Negative thinking?   Perhaps!
Or, is it maybe, just a loss of trust?
Why not just speak of the positive?
But, that position, mostly a bust!
Death is the doorway,

Life challenges, meeting them, a must for you to do!
If, I would be wrong;
And, life is on a better plain__
How ecstatic, I would be!
But, if what I say is right?
Can the good, "tie a can" to the Devil,
And, start a better world__ to see?

Do you understand?
Why and what I say
When, addressing, these words to thee?
Smile, you are on candid camera!
Is that a tear in your eye I see?

Question? Could you, be the "one"?
To, bring Brotherhood__ to everyone?
I wish: that could be?

But, remember__
Life is, what you make it__
Now, do you understand?
Now, do you see?

It is up to everyone__ that means, you and me!

Φ

Reminder!

There is a reason for snow! It piles up in the places around!
Some of course evaporates__ but the best;
Melts, into the earth below! Here, it provides, future moisture,
For the living! Nature's gift, on all__ does bestow!

Φ

Life Reviewed!

When in maturity, you realize,
It matters little, what your were,
But, with effort, what you will be!
It matters not, from whence you came,
But, where you go__
Throughout your life, that all can see!
It matters not how far,
Up the ladder, traveled you?
But, how many you reached down,
To help, raise up__ as some did you!
Forgiveness, for bad actions,
Some, will not extend,
But, if you know, how good you've became,
Then in your heart, free of debt, you are one!

These thoughts, for all, perhaps not true?
Because, some have set,
Vindictiveness, as a trap for you!
For, even if, you on water walked,
They would see you, as pictured before,
And, carry animus, to their death's door!
Tis, a shame,
Some, cannot see beyond their nose,
But this is life, and what__
Sometimes environment imposed!
So, I suggest this to one and all,
Learn early, to live the "Golden Rule",
Live it well, don't be the fool!
And, then less animosity, to you will accrue!
Sermon done, Amen!

Φ

Keep the 10% in Tact!

Learning must never stop!
Each new day, brings__
More to know, more to glean,
More to gather in your,
Thinking machine!

Now we know,
That energy in years is lost,
Pain, many times becomes the boss,
Loss of breath, sometimes even worse,
And, many diseases, become a curse!

But, the "tons of new",
Throughout our years does come__
Teasing our intellect, till the last?
To keep us young, like years before,
With knowledge ready, at the fore!

So, should more learning, be our goal?
Is it just to keep in touch?
Not so, for, if you stop;
Then, those who tend, to us__
Treat us like babies, they don't trust!

So, friend it is up to you__,
To stay or delay__ the aging process!
Exercise, that body you do possess,
Let learning each day, be your quest__
Keeping detractors, off balance__ so fun, you can digest!

Φ

Humankind on Trial!

Slavery, is an abomination,
That has sullied, many a Nation!
And, still takes place in this day and time,
Across, this world, we find!

Look thee, back in time,
Roman legion enslaved nations!
Arabs and Black enslaved other Blacks,
Hitler, enslave Gipsy, Jews and others!

Native Indians enslaved whites, and other tribes.
Criminals of all Nations,
Enslaved, youth to serve,
And, young women, made into concubines!
All this, even in our time!

In the year of twenty-seventeen,
Tempers flared, and things turned mean!
On, monuments of the Civil War,
Bantered slavery, which caused death,
And separation two centuries before!

150 plus, years of calendar pages had turned,
Since brother against brother,
Caused death and destruction,
And, a Nation, halved in turn!

And, the blame on one was heaped,
And, the reason and lies were deep!
But, there was much blame to go around,
Take a moment, and maybe truth be found!

Lets go back to 1776, and before,
When fathers founding,
A new Nation, were trying to score,
And this good, now marred, when reason carved!

Yes, a simple truth be brought forth,
To make a Nation,
Away from England's shores,
North and South__ slavery allowed!

Could they not remember?
For seven or more years proscribed!
Englishmen were indentured,
Another name for slavery, connived!

And, fortunes were built,
On, the backs of Blacks;
Both north and south,
Their coinage tracked!

So, not one is good and the other bad,
Both are bad, for slaves were had!
And, both for economics, fought a Civil war,
All men are equal, was a lie they scored!

Yes, those known as the "Slave States."
For, an additional plus seventy years.
Held in bondage, both man and woman,
Split families, and brought millions to tears!

And, even when before,
The end of war, and Slavery no more__
Fought that race in Yankee blue,
But, freedom, eluded them__
For another 100 years and a few!

And, there are even those today,
Who in their stupidity,
Who, on speaking of a minority, say__
We are better then they!

These are they,
Who, should be "put away,"
Never more to see the light of day,
For, their bias is poison delayed!

Tis, easy to dislike one you don't know,
Or, to cast all in a pot to stir,
Or, to even think you are,
Better, then him and her!

But, there is mostly,
More good than bad,
In all races, if an open mind be had!
And, the chance for talent, to come too the fore!

But, even now, there are those,
Who misguided__ suppose,
They now are owed?
For, what on others__ was imposed?

That is water over the dam,
For a century of death,
Has claimed the chain clinking man!
And, citizens today have no monetary demand!

So, as hard as it might seem,
Honest judging must be the theme,
And, all sides must together work,
For a land, where brotherhood can be seen!

Where together, hand in hand,
We can address and cure,
The divide, in each race and clan,
And assure, all humankind, can together stand!
Amen!

Ф

Is the Past the Future?

What we see in a telescope,
The beginnings of our universe,
A history of earth and man!
Did happen, millenniums before,

Locked in the distance it travels,
A chance for us to learn more!
Will future humankind, be around?
And, allowed to read, the next chapter scored?

Or, will the universe pull the plug?
Or is there God or the Devil,
Who, deems humans unfit anymore?
And, then with a word__ the Earth do destroy?

Was, Humankind an experiment gone wrong?
Or, is there a chance, another effort to employ?
What a world we live in today!
Can we make it better? What do you say?

Ф

A Change of Pace!
A Sextet of Verses, to Honor a Seasonal Space!

#1 Christmas Twenty-Seventeen

The days were rushing by,
Few were left, till "the sled", would fly,
The Eve, now just a day away,
Will, kids this year, have a Christmas Day?
For, Santa was down with a case of flu,
North Pole folks worried, and anxious too,

Would Santa be well enough?
His, flight to take, this year to do?
It was true! It, was, true!
Santa was abed, with the flu!
What to do! What, to do?
Elmer, the elf__ was in a stew!

The reindeer, felt the tension,
They were off their feed!
Never before had Santa missed,
The trip on Christmas Eve!
"Oh my, oh my, Santa moaned,
Why me, I don't want to stay at home!"

His stomach churned, his head did spin,
"I think this year I must stay in!"
Then__ the word did spread,
Not too worry, not to pout!
The toys and reindeer,
In the sleigh, would, get about?
Who, this rumor, did start?
What game was this to shout?

Would kids truly have a Christmas?
Would the toys_ be on their way?
True, the sleigh was primed and ready,
The reindeer were prancing about,
Rudolph had polished his nose,
And the Elves, let out a shout!
Why, there was Santa_
To the sled, he waddled down!

He climbed into the seat,
And, Elmer too, sat on down!
But, those that looked more closely,
Saw, it wasn't Santa at all!
But, Mrs. Clause in suit of red,
And, waving to one and all!
What a woman, what a gal!
She took the reins, and let out a call!

And, all heard loud and clear,
"Let's go Rudolph, lets spread Christmas cheer!"
And, each kid was visited,
And, Elmer did his thing_
And, Mrs. Clause was a huge success,
And, Santa so sick; he didn't know a thing!
Mrs. Clause felt pretty darn good,
And, Elmer smiled happily too!
They, both wished all; a Merry Christmas,
& Happy Holidays, before the morning dew!

Then, from somewhere out in space?
Was perhaps, the Master's voice?
"God Bless the women of this world,
Who keep humankind, on their course!"
HAPPY NEW YEAR!

Φ

#2 My Christmas Confession

I love to look at Christmas lights,
And, decorations, those pretty sights!
Their colors they stir my soul,
When the talent of others, is on a roll!

I recognize the work put in,
The hours it takes a scene to spin,
But, I have no love to impose,
A lack in me, I do suppose!

To me, decorating is a futile play,
All that work for a short, short stay!
To put it up and take it down,
I'd rather watch, as Egg Nog__ down!
Again, let me state
The finished beauty, I appreciate!
It's just that decorating is not my fate,
Thank God, others love that state!

So I will walk many streets,
And look at houses as they compete!
And, in malls colored sweet,
And, give greetings, to all I meet!

But, that is as far,
As my Psyche does prevail,
But don't, treat me hard,
For that, is my travail!

So to each and all,
Christian or not,
I smile and nod a lot,
Tis a holiday - for adult and tots!
The true reason for this,
I learned when young,
Tis written in my bible, some;
Of birth in a manger, and phrases sung!

So as Santa__ departs roof tops,
As the world he goes about,
I echo his sentiments,
I say them loud__ with a shout!

Merry Christmas, or Happy Holidays, & a prosperous New Year,
To all__ whether far or near!

Φ

#3
Natures,
Xmas Song!
Oh Christmas tree,
Oh Christmas tree,
In verses they do say!
Your beauty undeniable,
For, the season you do stay!
But why do, we cut you down?
Instead, of, bagging, roots found?
So, when you finish, your Xmas tour?
To nature,
Can be restored,
Into God's great outdoors¬!

Φ

#4 THE CHRISTMAS GIFT

I heard this somewhere__ I think?
About a family whose tardiness, was pure stink!
Not my family, of course; but, enjoy the verse & its voice!
For it is a lesson, perhaps make you to rejoice?

Enclosed within,
This envelope mine,
Is, a rather large check?
You will surely find?

Tis for Christmas,
And birthdays, 4 in the house
So cash it real quick,
Don't be a mouse!

Now listen my friend,
If the check isn't cashed,
The bottoms of all "four',
Will be thoroughly thrashed!

And then hence forth,
To the end of our time,
Your gift will be pennies
To count and divide!

They will be weighed,
So, the amount will be known,
But, the counting and wrapping
Will be your task alone!

This certainly will be,
My revenge and delight,
As I dream of you and yours,
Counting late in the night!

So with the Holiday upon us,
And birthdays quite near,
Honor my "request",
Out of love not fear!

But nothing, is as frustrating,
As, a check not cashed?
Unless its green dollars,
Which, were never stashed!

Φ

#5 BELIEF!

Perhaps you don't believe
And that is sure__ ok,
Perhaps it is only your conviction,
That keeps "old" Santa away,
But, perhaps if you just smile a bit,
As kids with each other play,

Perhaps because of Santa,
Tomorrow will be a better day?
If Santa can make life better,
Let's not keep his act__ away!
The world hasn't done a very good job,
So maybe, Santa can bring peace__ on Earth to stay?

Φ

#6 One Christmas Eve Night!

Santa was sitting in his sleigh,
Scratching his beard of white!
Thinking, what the heck, am I supposed to do__?
On this, one of winter's coldest snowy nights!

Those Reindeer? Hitched up to this sled?
And me in a red suit, that's too tight!
A red suit; have a lost my mind?
Did I have too much to drink tonight?

Where the heck are my glasses?
I can't see the GPS without any sight?
And why am I sitting in a sleigh?
Is my Mercedes, parked just out of the light?

Why won't the cops come get me?
I can sleep it off in a drunk-tank – right?
And maybe then by mid-morning,
This nightmare will be just__ a moment of fright!

What was in that Turkey sandwich?
Or was it in the punch so red and bright?
Who was that woman, who was cuddling?
Did the Mrs.' see that tonight?

What the "hey" is happening?
Did aliens take me on a flight?
Who in the heck am I?
And why have I a beard that's snowy white!

What I need is the "hair of the Dog",
To bring my memory back!
Or am I dead and buried?
Is the Devil, playing a game, out of spite?

Santa made a move to get out of the sleigh,
But, fell and hit his head a lick,
And when he was fully conscious,
His memory came back real quick!

"Those darn elves he thought,
Put something in my punch!
Look at them up there laughing,
I should have never trusted that bunch!"

So Santa got back in the sleigh,
And, drank strong coffee__ Mrs. Clause gave!
He snapped the reins, at the laughing reindeer,
And swore, no more "Elf- Punch" would he crave!

Φ

Ah, Seasons Four, nature has made it so,
You can pick the one you like best,
But, verse, music and some religions,
Has made one to stand out so,
Thus, enjoy them all,
But make, the last calendar one__
The one, you will forever know!

Φ

Those Left Behind!
(A dedication to Kairos, who in Prisons Serve!)

Prayers I do say,
When Kairos is on its way,
As Missionaries fine__
To share time, with those behind bars!

They give of their time,
To help those,
Whose lives -
Have gone astray!

The saying of old,
Stated and bold,
"He works in mysterious ways,"
They of Kairos, follow his command!

And, then, as a band,
Spreading his word,
Taking a stand, to help those,
That bars, do command!

So falter you not,
As to prisons you trot,
Be assure, God's word__
Will make better each man!

And should you not get all,
Let your spirit not fall,
For you plant in faith,
That too, is God's Command!

What, makes one,
To follow the sun,
While, others go far astray?
To, spend wasted time each day!

What, makes most,
Of prisons they boast,
Make you, to spend time,
To, assure them a better day?

What guides you, -
Through Kairos to view,
Spending time locked in,
There may be a better way?

Like you, my prayer for all,
Is to hear the Bible's call!
And my favorite verse,
Be the Golden Rule__

If but we do unto others,
As we would have them do,
Then perhaps those of Kairos,
Can assure, for them a better life to view!

Φ

Just a Thought!

It is tough to see changing times,
And, to be too old, to play a part,
Yet, too young to bide my time,
Is there a new game, I dare to start?

Φ

City Kid!

When you are a kid, from Baltimore Town,
Every open lot; is a ball field found!
And back alley's__ were a place to play__
Tin-Can Jimmy or duck on a rock!
That is when they can be used__
When not traversed by,
Trash, or garbage trucks,
Or, ice trucks, or seafood vendors,
Or A-rabs, selling vegetables and stuff!

And, there were duels,
With wooden swords!
And, rubber band guns,
With inner-tube__ ammo,
Stretched for rifle multi shots,
Or pistols with one, to hit and run!

And, marbles, played,
On the old school grounds!
And, pitching baseball cards,
Against any house wall found,
And, the Catholic Church's,
Rounded fence wall, a great place,
To bounce a tennis ball!
And lets not forget, Tray-ball__
Batted with an old-broom stick!

And monopoly boards,
With deeds & money spread,
In someone's backyard, on a summer day!
And, night time near,
The gas, street light; lit!
Playing leapfrog, and hook and ladder__
While clinging, to the pole ever so dear!

And, across alleys, between houses,
Where side walks allowed,
Challenging "red rover to come over."
And other games played proud!

Or trips to Mooney's woods,
For tadpoles and stuff!
Or, on to the "stock yards,"
To see the pigs and steers,
And horses, rodeo stock!
And, over to the Iron Metal Company,
To see so much great stuff!

And Christmas day, with buddies to see,
And, many presents, to ogle under the tree!
Trains in gardens, in Fire Houses too.
Then Easter after church; butting dyed eggs to do!

And, when the snow did fly,
Snow balls fights,
Snow forts and igloos too!
Sledding down hills,
Till time to go home, for cocoa__
While, wet clothes were reviewed!

And, always a warning from Mom,
Just be careful when crossing the street,
And, be home for dinner on time,
When you dad, wants to eat!
And, for Pete's sake be good,
You know__ I love you!

And, that first two-wheeler,
And, roller skates strapped on!
And, orange crate scooters,
With old skates on a 2 x 4s, nailed on!

And, football under the lights,
On Westinghouse's grass!
When fall nights did come!
And, other great stuff, we gingered up!

No television was needed,
No I-pads, no-internet to rebuff!
Just kids, learning and growing,
And doing all kind of stuff,
You walked to school, in my neighborhood,
And, back home for lunch,
And back then again__
Our teachers, there to welcome__ us in!

Then Jr. High; teen years begun!
And, even after High School,
I found, it was the Elementary Years,
And freedom, I truly, found "cool!"

Growing then, just after the War,
When doors stayed unlocked,
And, neighbor's yards and houses,
Were, second –homes!
And, all of the above just scratched__
The surface, of life then known,
A time, I doubt kids, ever see again!
Too bad, they, won't know__
But, believe, what they have now,
Was, how we lived__ then!

There are many days__ when I wish, I were that kid again,
Just, for a time to relive, that life back then!

Φ

A Boat!

I bought a boat the other day,
Some did say, "you are nuts,"
Just throwing money away!"
What they didn't, give me a chance to say,
It was just a model; that caught my eye_
A replica of a dream, long gone by!

If afloat, and for real,
Sixty plus feet, her length would be,
Her mast, at least as high,
Her keel ¾ of her hull,
Copied from a "J" boat_ I do feel,
Not, a schooner, always my desire,
But a sloop with two head- sails!
A reminder, of a boat,
That passed me by!
So for a couple of bucks,
I do see, and my memory jogs,
Of a time, I wore sailor's togs!
And, while on water many times,
I never, caught either, dream of mine!
Oh, how now, I wish I could claim,
A chance to grab that dream again!
Be, it too late now, a dream to catch?

I hope your dreams, you can fetch!
But, unlike me, when only loss was met!
Today, good memories of other things,
Keeps me happy, no, sadness rings,
Of things now lost forever; maybe seen_
Isn't that the purpose of a dream?

Φ

Nonsensical, Suppositions!

Sunset seen, tis the end of day!
Don't we agree__ it has always been that way?
But, just suppose, storm clouds, hide the sun away!
Does our day__ then, not end?
Just because we see not the sun__
Dropping below the horizon, west again?

Or, does it travel through,
The time of night,
When the moon is due?
Or, just because we see not,
The sun drop out of sight,
Does, day remain and there is no night?

Does it make a bit of difference?
Between vision and sight,
The vision of sun down,
Bringing forth the sight of night?

Or is it the clock,
That turns day into night?
And, has nothing to do__
With, the sun's orbital; flight?

And, do we need a clock?
Or, the sun, to take stock__
What would you say__ if we had no sun!
And, we had no clock?
Just black! In the morning and night?
No light; just black, and black, and black!

Who, would tell us when it is day__
And, also when is night?

Would there be a morning,
If the sun gave no warning,
And, refused to make its flight?

Could we live__ in perpetual dark,
Needing no eyes, because there was no spark?
And, the whole damn planet;
Spinning, with not a shaft of light?

Could we call that day?
Or do we call that night?

Just a few thoughts,
To tempt your mind!
So, ask I,
What idea__ could you get behind?
Well, maybe not behind__
But in front, too pull the sun behind!

Do you think the sun?
Will, always__ light this sphere?
Or, are these words,
A forecast__ of a future we need to fear?

Funny, what an ounce of marijuana__
Can do, to thoughts, you once held dear!
Good morning sun! Bye, bye sunset,
Hello night! Welcome moon, is the sun in sight?

All nonsense maybe, but could some of it be right?

Φ

Of a Man Known!

There once was a day,
As the time passed away,
I got to thinking,
What, I was to do?

So, I packed up my bag,
With much of my swag,
And, boarded a "Greyhound"__
To broaden my view!
This wasn't a mistake,
But, a chance I did take,
To open my mind,
To the world, I never knew!

And, traveled__ I did,
To many, places I'd not known!
And, knowledge I gained,
Never to have gotten__ in college alone!

So, I went on my way,
Trying, varied experiences__ each day,
Like jobs, gangs, things unnamed,
Each, a part of the person, now I claim!
I spent a spell on a trawler,
Fishing cod, tuna, and the like!
Digging, in a mine,
For coal to help, my country to light!

I spent some years in the army,
Carrying, a rifle, with ammo__ used!
And, pushed a pencil,
Tracking, accounts overdue!

Then spent time "hopping" trains,
And, visiting towns, I now, can't name!
And, sailing in the Caribbean,
Sipping rum, in the sunshine gained!
Then back to college some,
After, many years a diploma won!
And a steady job and place,
Then married, kids grown and on their own!

Now, the point__ I subscribe,
If you, are to live, and truly be alive?
You__ must find, what the world can provide,
So, in one place only__ you cannot reside!

For, most schools, teach you not,
The basics of living a lot!
Like, keeping a checkbook correct!
Tis, knowledge of the world, life reflects!
Now, I don't know about you?
But, what these verses say true__
It takes time traveling the Earth, to exact__
The very best in life, you can attract!

So, take it or leave it!
These thoughts, I share with you!
And, should you go another way,
I pray, "Lady Luck"__ be most kind to you!

Φ

Rainbows have no pot of gold, but their beauty does unfold__
After a rain to nourish the earth, a double treat, to quench your thirst!

Φ

Doubling Down!

There comes a time,
In life realized,
When "doubling down" is no surprise,
The mirror tells you,
That the fact is true__
That your youth is gone,
And middle age is leaving too!

You see your kids,
And, your friend's kids too,
All have the forty+ mark__ well in view!
Your hair is now graying__
Wasn't it yesterday__ that love was new?

Now maybe your age,
Perhaps, a quarter century more then they,
But, you're pushing hard, each new day,
And, while there is much you'd like to do,
You realize__ retirement is soon in view!

But there is nothing to fear,
In these days still ahead,
If, you have lived more good,
Then bad, in life, you did!
For, this is Mother Nature, doing her thing,
And, it is the same__ for Prince or King!

So look the future in the eye,
Take it on, don't pass it bye,
Tis, just another challenge to try,
Be you, a gal or guy!

Maybe, this is a "downer" for you?
That, to face up to the future__
Is not what you want to do?
That you want nothing but surprises,
And, no complications__ ever in view!
I ask__ what is the matter with you?

There are no promises made at birth,
Kicking and screaming you're placed on earth!
Most have parents to guide them through,
Till teenage years to them are due!
And then to seek, with help on your way,
For, tis soon__ for you,
To guide others, to that new and shining day!

And, now most years have passed on by,
True, there are still many left to try!
So, give it your all__ each morn you rise!
Improve, your legacy, don't let it die,
And, "doubling down" is truly a prize!

So, make each day the best you can,
Watch your diet, and active be!
Go see what the world has to offer you?
Even try, a new vocation if you please,
Hold on tightly, for the best yet can be!
For, it's how you "live" the Golden Years,
That will keep you in smiles, and not tears!

Φ

A Timely Thought!

This day is lost, and, so am I!
Somewhere under, this vast blue sky,
What, has happened to me?

No, knowledge, can I now gain,
That, doesn't bring more, sadness and pain!
Where, am I now?
And, who can I be?

More poignant, then, than knowing,
I was unable, too in any why,
To help change,
My, country's, history__ at play!

So, much__ so much, needs be done!
To return us, from adversity__
And once again, be the nation__
Of diversity, for each and everyone!!

Is it too late, as others, in history?
That faced, a similar fate?
Oh, God in Heaven,
Guide us, before it is too late!

"My country tis of thee",
My prayers to God,
I send for thee,
Let us again become,
"Sweet land of Liberty!"

Φ

Question?

If one knew, from day of birth__
The actual day, of one's demise?
Would, one's life, take on,
A different, aspect__
Then, just living daily__ to survive?

What, if you could, choices make?
To live as now, till death does overtake?
Or would you make a better life__
Knowing just when, your last breath take?
Which choice__ would you make?
An option, to explore!

Φ

Pain Be Real!

The worse to "recall," is things untried!
Knowing, __ you missed a chance that arrived!
Having missed it, & never to know__
What, the outcome__ just might bestow?

Yes, untried things, leaves a void within__
A cut; maybe, near impossible to heal?
An opportunity, never again, to be real!

If in life, you do take the chance?
Win or loose__ an answer is found,
Glad, I took that road__ to go down!

Φ

To Each Ones' Own!

Life is an experiment to do!
How much accomplished, is up to you!
Does not matter, what challenge, is named__
All; tries, are measured__ by gain!

But, the effort, you maintain__
When, an idea; goes up__ in flames,
To start over again, is a true measure__
Of, the "pluck" you can claim!

For, God is a miser of sorts,
He gives only so much away!
Then__ it's your brain, and effort sustained,
To adapt, and succeed__ on a given day!

Not, all things you do; will a success, be unto you!

But, that is the game__ life plays!
So whatever your choice,
If be a bust__ never, give up too soon,
For then__ only frustration is heaped upon you!

So, lets take a moment__ to review!
For, all things, you see as prime__
Take study, research, & time!
And, a work ethic, to subscribe!

But perhaps, if a partner you dare?
The effort by two; be a success!
Also know, that there is more to life__
Then being a tyrant, in the field you profess!

Better to be nice and liked, and seen__
As, truly a good person, to be near,
One, who helps others, whose path is not clear!
Many can die, holding, dollars and cents,
Not loved, is one who is feared!

To live well, on your time on Earth,
Which, was a gift, granted to you__
Is, truly a challenge an enigma_
Wrapped in a puzzle, a true conundrum,
Too face__ daily by you!

Φ

Your Choice!

Worry not the hours you have remaining--
For, there is one, keeping track for you!
But rather, concern yourself__
With your time left__ that, it's only good, you do!

If you do not, read the Bible each day?
You are in the majority!
But, that thing inside__ called "conscience",
Is "God's" reminder__ doing good, is your priority!

This is not saying, church and God,
Are not needed by you?
But rather, heed your conscience__
And, live the Golden Rule!

Φ

Gratitude & Sorrow!

Grateful am I, for verse I pen,
And, nice words I hear in praise!

And, glad too, that I can aid,
Not-For-Profit organizations,
Using my books, to acquire funds,
For, what they promise can be done!

To write, I did in my professional life,
And, while verse over the years did pen,
It wasn't until my "bride" did pass,
That more writing and publishing,
For others to read, I did extend!

My wife knew some bits of my verse,
On Christmas, letters I wrote!
But, even she would have been surprised,
At the amount I write, but never orally quote!

There is a deep sadness, I always feel,
That verse, I started so late,
That my wife, and folks,
Never, my books could appreciate!

But, thankful am I,
My "Master,"
Fills my mind with words to quote!
And, I can be his scribe,
And, pray people are helped,
With, the verses, I write and wrote!

Φ

Then and Now!

I was taught to believe in Sunshine,
That it would be with me all the time!
Sure there would be rain drops,
To dampen farm fields,
And, woodlands, across this earth so fine!

But, it is the sunshine, from "Father Sun,"
That keeps this world from dying,
While, all in the universe__ is endlessly spun,
And, "The Sun" with it's gravity,
Holds planets, in their orbit__ from be flung!

And now, that I have given thought__
I, sense there is more; then that,
That makes__ all life possible __
Where ever "life is at"!
Perhaps, it is God, who I shall ask__ about that?

What a place was this Earth!
In a time before man__ laid on his curse,
But, perhaps, when he is gone,
The devastation, will be put in reverse,
And, Earth again, will be, a place of worth!

So, what do you think?
Of, the rhyming lines scribed above?
Do they, cause you__ to opine?
Is, there, truth in every line?
Or think you the "world and man" are fine?

"Man, who sees, but takes not note__ is blind, with sight or not!"

Φ

Death be Damned!

I met a man by chance,
No choice did I have?
Fate, was the interlocutor; of this "date",
A spawn of the devil, not my mate!

It was where no human could equate,
A road, flat and wide,
With no traffic in sight,
Just two vehicles, out for the ride!

I was driving from one State to another,
My eyes on the road,
My mind, on quandaries, to abide,
Grey cold clouds _ in winter's mode!

The first I knew, when a horn blew!
It jolted me alive,
The rear view mirror,
Captured an auto, hard to describe!

Slick, black, low to the road,
Turbo pipes, shine of silver's glint,
A mask on a face, eyes maniac bright,
Mouthing words, "let's race tonight?

Across the solid line,
The driver, now beside the car of mine,
Engine gunning, challenging me!
His car a beauty, his face, death to see!

Was this race, a place__?
I wanted to be?
Or was this__ a death wish,
He, the Devil; tempting me!

Well, we raced that night,
And, I will bore you not,
But miles we covered,
Till morning's light!

And, out of fuel, my engine stopped,
Then out of his car,
His body popped,
And, he was the devil_ incarnate!

He smiled at me, and said "not yet!"
"But, I will be waiting for thee!"
And, a voice we, heard, from afar!
"Not this one, he's mine you see!

And from the sky,
A clap of thunder so loud,
Then, came lightening bright,
And, the devil disappeared from view!

Finally, fully awake, my heart pounding,
Body drenched in sweat
Had this been but a dream?
Or was this a presage, of a future seen?

Has a dream like this_ ever visited you?
Tis, in truth, it is a lesson told!
That perhaps, if you live by "Golden Rule,"
The Devil_ will be avoiding you!

Φ

To Listen!

Reviewing life, is a game, I play,
Today, it's classical music__
Stirred by The "Christmas Ballet"!
Brought back thoughts, of college days,
When Music Appreciation;
Freshmen, no choice__ was a class to stay!

Music Appreciation, I said "Oh Hell",
But, tis the course, I appreciated most today!
No instrument, can I play__
Unless you consider, time on the harmonica,
Tunes, I try to convey?
But, music, all types, I do enjoy,

"Why the Classics", I hear you ask?
Because, of there technical genius,
And, the beauty they bring to the craft,
Their ability, a story, an epic to write,
From first note to last,
Not, a ditty, but a masterpiece, in it's own right!

I can just sit and listen,
As, each instrument, plays its part,
The intricacies, of their entrance,
The magic when they know to depart,
The talent playing, in a symphony Hall__
Hundreds of years, of total practice time,
Just, to take a small part__ in music so sublime!

I send gratitude to those, who bring ecstasy?
To the world, either in concert, or a disc to see

And, be honest I will,
Be it Hayden, or Bach, or
Another master of gone-by years!
As an early riser, that_ I am,
I employ, as, an aid to my thinking!
Of verse, God helps me write,

Those classics, I so enjoy!
In early morning or when ever right!
I beg you take the time,
If this, you have not done?
Open up your ears and your mind,
And hear, what I now hear!

The work of the composers,
Of those ages passed by,
There brilliance of phrasing,
Then, delight in the music,
As each instrument,
It's voice does supply!

Of course, if have, listened through life_
I tell you, little you don't already know!
But urge you_ to take, a novice, in hand_
And, invite them as your guest,
The very next time_
There is a symphony, at your command!

Ф

Why!

It, seems to happen to all?
In time, when ageing makes a call__
That seconds, minutes and days fly by!
What be the reason?
No rationale can one, apply?
But gone, is that portion of time,
Fast, faster, it boggles the mind!
Few, will hazard, even a guess__ just why?
So, memory becomes the collector,
The savior, of things gone by!
Available from the mind,
When, recall is applied!
But, the challenge is to keep those moments,
Whole and true__
Not letting, wishes,
Replace facts, with lies untrue!

One can buy, apples and oranges,
Houses and cars, and unlimited things__
But, time perhaps allocated?
Once gone, is an un-purchasable thing!
And, yet, most do treat "time," as renewable?
And, available at ones every whim!
Until__ it is too late,
And, one feels__ death's sting!
Time, what a gift!
This measureable thing!
Tis sometimes paused, if deviltry does lurk!
And, the, heart, might restart with a jerk!
But, do hear this,
To use it not__ judicially,
Then, God's gift, of this glorious thing__
Is wasted and gone, like, the dying of a wind!

Φ

From the Vineyard!

"Wine," perhaps,
Is, the most ancient of brews?
Who is to truly to know?
Beer drinkers __ say not so!

But, wine not over-done, Touches, the tongue with love,
And, continues, its caress, when, the pallet has none!

Tis, good for the heart,
For the psyche__ is divine,
Never in excess__
Then, a, partnership__ best of kind!

The beverage of dreams, sharpens, the taste buds__
Of, all foods__ it finds! Choice, of the Gods!

Not all, will ever understand,
The fascination of fruit__
From the tree, and the vine,
That fills the winemakers mind!

Tis, up to the individual, to determine the taste__
If it be port, or Chardonnay, or others__ that be their kind!

Have a goblet! Make a toast!
Share a carafe! Take a sip!
Ask a sommelier to help,
Your taste to refine!

Knowing wines, a test to learn, but more__
Than worth the time! A bouquet, for an aroma__ sublime!

Φ

Facing Life!

I, knew at an age,
My, weaknesses well!
And, also knew,
I would/could_ few, expel!

I am sure, all have faced,
The moment, when_
No choice was to be had?
How one's life, was better to spend?

To face dark secrets, well, known?
Long submerged, but now_
Risen, to face all demons,
And, the future_ in which to excel!

So, I sit and reviewed,
What for tomorrows, I had to do!
I knew, the world's full battles___
That, many, I would exclude!

And, ride without, not within!
Those weaknesses_ I had,
I could no longer abide!
If in the future, I was never to hide!

Twas then, my psyche,
Pointed out to me,
See, hear, watch, and learn,
Take the time and be!

Then too, realization__
Came strongly to me,
Knowing things will__ would,
Come, more slowly to me!

Never, in the 1% __
Be a place fitting for me!
Because, happy there__
I could not ever be!

Too many skills, in me lacking,
Too, much honesty,
Too much empathy,
In me resides!

But, like many, in my life,
And in most likely yours__
Hard work and determination:
Was a trait, I much adored!

To keep the country strong,
To live the Golden Rule,
To save what you can,
To raise your children right!

Then, some success, will you get!
And, for most,
That__ be a dream well met!
And, a life full__ with little to regret!

Φ

Music of its Time!

How did I miss so much?
And, wonder, how, and why?
I now listen to the talent,
There, in my day__ now 40 years by!

That music now touches my soul!
Where was I, when it was fresh and new?
Time I wasted; those years gone by?
Dancing "The Last Waltz", my sadness grew!

Now 40 years hence,
"The Band," now gone, four decades thence!
What talent lost to time!
That, talent now captured in my mind!

First the "Hawk", then as "The Band."
Reputation recognized, on this earthly land!
But, unfortunately not then by me!
ABBA, now gone, only on disc, to find!

I rationalize__ I, was busy as a bee,
With, family, and, debts to pay,
While, on NPR, news shorts, I did hear!
All__ kept me busy, till retirement day!

Now aging,
I listen with an open ear,
And shed tears,
That long ago__ I didn't hear!

Φ

A, Thought to Think!

We were wed 7 years,
Before our first child, did arrive!
Seven long years, many test to survive!
He was a welcome addition,
But, if we knew, what his life would be,
On another choice__ we both might agree!
My bride, had taken a medication,
To make the fetus, adhere!
But, what awaited, that boy of ours, born__
Was, suffering__ his every single year!

A, drug, too late, for a cure to make!
Far too late, for our son, Jay!
Died not young, as predicted,
But, no real life, worth the stay!
With death not until his 48th year!
His ashes now do rest__
In his loving mothers arms!
In a grave, I will join with them,
When God, thinks I am worthy,
To be near!

I tell you this truth, so wisely__
You think__ before decisions make!
How they not only affect you?
But, on all, whom your judgment__ takes!
And, when I bend my head to pray,
I ask my son's forgiveness,
For the pain__ in love,
We brought him, every living day!

Φ

Pros & Cons!

When you, pick up something to read,
And, your anger, nothing will impede!

Because, those words, stimulate your ire!
So, read more for sure!

For many times the writer,
Plays, the devil's advocate, to test your core?

And, in a place or piece, forward on__
He or she, opens, the other door!

This depends on the writer of course,
For, if always, one side, only is discussed?
This writer; is a bust__ a prejudiced, biased, hack!

Who clutters his/her mind!
Leaving, many times, truth behind!
And, no room__ for real truth to find!

So, be sure,
YOU, look at both sides of the coin!
For you just might, one day recognize__

You were supporting, the wrong idea?
With, your-thinking, your bias, and, your time!
Just a thought__ to keep your faculties in line"

Φ

Words Never Said!

I think, about the folks I knew,
Not, when they were young, that's true,
But, when they were my mentors fine,
　　In the years, I came up the line!

Now, when, old photos, if I see,
Their younger faces smile at me,
As, though, they, then did know,
　　Someday, their wisdom__
On me__ they would bestow!

This day, I looked at photos of some,
　　A, potpourri spread in time,
　It was as if, I knew them well,
　　And, my respect and love,
　　　For them, does swell!

　　Yes, now I am aging too,
　　　I appreciate them more,
　　Then, I can ever tell!
And truly hope someday, in__
Others for me, that feeling will dwell!

But these, those mentors of mine,
Who cared not, for fame to find!
Are from this world, now gone,
Like so many others, who taught__
And, are now, silently enshrined,
In every student's mind__ forever more!

Ф

Benediction for Boaters!
(Or with words adapted, a prayer for all!)

As the bell it tolls, thus ending
Another watch__ we bid ado!
We bow our heads in reverence,
And, send our pray to you.

We beg you guide us safely,
To our ports, where ere they be!
We ask for peace, for all nations,
Rather, then war to see!

We ask that you help the hungry,
The halt, the lame, the poor!
And, all who suffer life's challenges,
Give them strength, so they can endure!

We ask for good health, oh Master,
To, better serve thy will!
And, open our hearts to others,
And, let empathy good deeds instill!

We ask you give us patience,
To see good at every door,
And, to make decisions wisely,
As, through life__ we explore!

We send to you our gratitude,
For, your many blessing shared!
And beg you, bless this nation o' father,
And, us to thy will declared!

Φ

FINIS!

www.ingramcontent.com/pod-product-compliance
Lightning Source LLC
Chambersburg PA
CBHW060204050426
42446CB00013B/2986